THE ELEMENTS

Nickel

Giles Sparrow

Benchmark Books
Marshall Cavendish
99 White Plains Road
Tarrytown, New York 10591

www.marshallcavendish.com

Library of Congress Cataloging-in-Publication Data

Sparrow, Giles.
Nickel / Giles Sparrow.
p.   cm. — (The elements)
Includes index.

ISBN 0-7614-1811-3
1. Nickel—Juvenile literature. I. Title. II.
Elements (Benchmark Books)
QD181.N6S63 2005
546'.625—dc22

2004047643

Printed in China

Picture credits
Front cover: Atlantic Metals & Alloys
Back cover: QNI Pty Ltd

Anglo American: 13, 14
ARS: Keith Weller 19
Atlantic Metals & Alloys: 4
BHP Billiton: 30
Corbis: Jack Fields 3, 9, Dan Guravich 24, Ted Spiegel 10
IBM Corporation: 5
Photos.com: 22
QNI Pty Ltd: 12, 15, 20
Rolls Royce Plc: 23
Science & Society Picture Library: Science Museum 11
Science Photo Library: Dr. P. Marazzi 27, Jerry Mason 16
Special Metals Corporation: 1, 7, 17
The Royal Coin Cabinet, Stockholm, Sweden: 8
United States Mint: 26
US Department of Defense: 21

Series created by The Brown Reference Group plc.
Designed by Sarah Williams
www.brownreference.com

Contents

What is nickel?

Nickel is a silver-white metal that is used in a variety of industries. In our everyday lives, we are most likely to encounter nickel in coins and stainless steel products. Nickel is also an important part of many high-tech devices.

Nickel is rarely found as a pure metal in nature. The element itself was only discovered in the eighteenth century. Instead, nickel is found in chemical compounds and minerals called ores. Nickel ores are often green or red.

Atomic structure

Like all elements, individual nickel atoms are composed of even smaller particles. Most of an atom's mass is contained in a tiny nucleus at its center. The nucleus is made of particles called protons and neutrons. Protons have a positive electric charge. Neutrons have no charge but have the same mass as the protons. Smaller particles called electrons orbit the nucleus. They have almost no mass but a negative

Pure nickel is rarely found in nature. This metal has been purified from a type of rock called an ore. Nickel is generally used mixed with other metals.

DID YOU KNOW?

ORIGINAL NAME

Nickel gets its name from the old German name *kupfernickel*, which translates as "Nick's copper." Miners gave it that name when they were looking for copper-bearing rocks and instead found what they thought was a useless waste material. The "Nick" that the copper belonged to was probably "Old Nick"— a traditional name for the devil.

electric charge equal to a proton's positive charge. Atoms carry no overall electrical charge. The numbers of electrons and protons in an atom are always equal and their charges are canceled out. In nickel, 28 protons are held in the nucleus

The surface of a piece of nickel seen with a high-powered electron microscope. Each dome represents an individual nickel atom.

and 28 electrons orbit around them. Each element has a unique number of protons or electrons. This is called its atomic number. Nickel's atomic number is 28.

Isotopes

The rest of the atom is made up of neutrons. All atoms of nickel have the same number of protons, but there are several different forms of the element with different numbers of neutrons. These different forms are called isotopes. Each isotope has a slightly different mass. The mass of an atom is measured in atomic mass units, which are equivalent to the mass of one proton or neutron. Nickel's different isotopes have masses of 58, 60, 61, 62, and 64. The official atomic mass of nickel is the average of all the isotopes. It is close to 59.

Electron shells

Elements take part in chemical reactions in which they gain or lose electrons. The reactions fill or empty the electron shells of atoms. Nickel is a transition metal like iron and copper. All transition metals have two electrons in their outer shell. (A nickel atom's outer shell can hold a maximum of eight particles.) During most of nickel's reactions, the atoms lose these two outer electrons. The nickel then forms bonds with the other elements that have accepted the electrons.

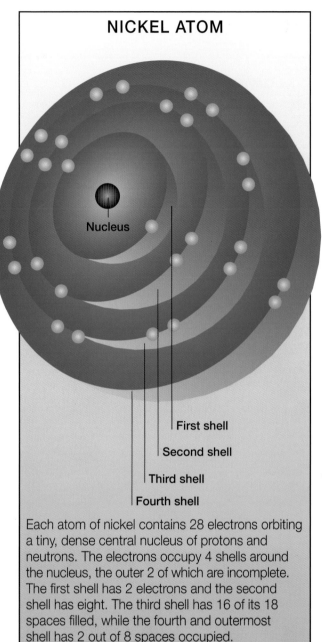

NICKEL ATOM

Nucleus

First shell

Second shell

Third shell

Fourth shell

Each atom of nickel contains 28 electrons orbiting a tiny, dense central nucleus of protons and neutrons. The electrons occupy 4 shells around the nucleus, the outer 2 of which are incomplete. The first shell has 2 electrons and the second shell has eight. The third shell has 16 of its 18 spaces filled, while the fourth and outermost shell has 2 out of 8 spaces occupied.

The inner shells of most elements are completely full of electrons. Like other transition metal, however, nickel atoms have an incomplete inner shell that can accept more electrons. This allows nickel to form very complex molecules.

Special characteristics

NICKEL FACTS	
Chemical symbol	Ni
Atomic number	28
Atomic mass	59
Melting point	2647 °F (1453 °C)
Boiling point	4950 °F (2732 °C)
Number of isotopes	5 stable isotopes

Elements in the periodic table are arranged according to their atomic number and behavior. Nickel's behavior shows similarities to its neighbors in the periodic table: Copper is on one side, and cobalt and iron are on the other. Platinum and palladium lie below it in the same column of the table.

In its pure form, nickel atoms form crystals in which each atom joins to six other nickel atoms. This arrangement means that the metal atoms can slide past each other easily when heated. This makes nickel a very ductile metal, which means it can be pulled into wires very easily.

Sea of electrons

The outer electrons in metal atoms are free to move around the whole crystal. This creates a "sea" of electrons that can flow through the metal easily, carrying an electric current. That is why nickel is a good conductor of electricity.

Another characteristic of nickel is its magnetism. Each nickel atom has two electrons in its unfilled inner shell. These make the atoms behave like tiny magnets. The inner shells overlap with those of neighboring atoms, and they all line up. This makes the nickel magnetic, and it is attracted to iron and a few other metals.

Nickel is a strong but ductile metal. This makes it useful for making a wide range of objects from pipes and plates to wires. Nickel is often mixed with other metals to make useful mixtures called alloys.

The history of nickel

DISCOVERERS

AXEL FREDERICK CRONSTEDT

Baron Axel Frederick Cronstedt was a pioneering mineralogist and chemist. He was among the first people to realize that the different forms of minerals were due to the chemicals they contained. He is best known today as the discoverer of nickel, but his new element was not immediately recognized. Many chemists found it hard to distinguish it from cobalt, which they already knew about.

Although its properties had been used for centuries, nickel was only identified as a metal and a separate element in the eighteenth century. In China's Yunan province, a mixture, or alloy, of nickel, copper, and zinc called *pai t'ung* was used as early as 1700 B.C.E. German miners used nickel ore called kupfernickel to color glass.

Nickel chemistry

The first chemist to properly investigate nickel was the Swedish scientist Axel Frederick Cronstedt (1722–1765). In 1751, he extracted the metal from a kupfernickel ore, mined in Germany. This ore is now called niccolite. Cronstedt showed that the metal had enough properties to be classified as a new element.

A nickel coin shows chemist Axel Frederick Cronstedt climbing down into a mine. His studies led to the discovery of nickel as a new element.

In 1804, German Jeremias B. Richter (1762–1807) succeeded in producing a much purer sample of nickel. He was able to assess its properties accurately for the first time. Around this time, European chemists discovered how to make alloys similar to the ancient Chinese pai t'ung. The mix of copper, nickel, and zinc produced a strong, silvery alloy that was easy to use. It was named nickel-silver despite the fact that it contained no silver. The inexpensive alloy was used for cutlery and other items that had previously been made from silver and other precious metals. Nickel-silver made

The remains of a nickel mine on the Pacific island of New Caledonia. Nickel has been mined there for nearly 150 years.

it possible for silver-colored luxury items to be available to less wealthy people.

Electroplating

Soon, chemists discovered a way of covering nickel-silver with a thin layer of real silver. This process is called electroplating. It involves passing electricity from a nickel-silver object to a block of silver. The nickel-silver and silver blocks are immersed in a silver solution. As electricity passes from the nickel to the silver, silver atoms move in the opposite direction and are laid down onto the nickel-silver object. The resulting items, known as electroplated nickel-silver, are still widely used today as an alternative to solid silver cutlery.

Other uses

As scientists invented and investigated new alloys, they soon realized the usefulness of nickel. The first nickel-based coins were introduced in the 1860s. The world's first large-scale mines opened on the South Pacific island of New Caledonia in 1876. In 1913 the first practical stainless steels, based on iron, chromium, and nickel, were introduced.

Until the late nineteenth century, nickel was hard to purify. German chemist Ludwig Mond (1839–1909) discovered that nickel combined with carbon monoxide gas (CO) to form a green gas called nickel tetracarbonyl—$Ni(CO)_4$. When this gas was burned, it released pure nickel. Carbonyls are still used to purify several metals, although other methods are used for refining nickel. Today, nickel is used in a range of technologies, and 1.75 million tons (1.6 million tonnes) are used a year.

Where nickel is found

A piece of nickel ore mined from the huge meteorite crater at Sudbury, Ontario. The metal is purified in a refinery next to the mine. The refinery releases a lot of pollution into the air.

Although nickel is more abundant than familiar metals like copper, it only makes up 0.007 percent of the material in Earth's crust. It is far more common deep inside Earth, where it is completely out of reach. The molten metal core at the center of Earth is made up of iron and between 7 and 10 percent nickel.

The reason for nickel's concentration at Earth's core is because it was common in the material that formed our planet and the rest of the Solar System, 4.5 billion years ago. But as tons of rock and dust particles collided to form our young planet, the Earth soon became completely

WORLD'S NICKEL RESERVES

There are about 58 million tons (52 million tonnes) of nickel ore reserves. These are distributed around the world.

●	Australia	34%
●	Russia	11%
●	North America	11%
●	Cuba	9%
●	New Caledonia	8%
●	Africa	6%
●	China	6%
●	Southeast Asia	6%
●	Europe	1%
●	South America	0.5%

molten (melted into a liquid). The heaviest elements within it, such as nickel and other metals, sank toward the center.

Nickel is still common today in the rocks that litter the Solar System and occasionally collide with Earth as meteorites. It seems that most of the nickel on Earth's surface today ended up there when rocks from space collided with Earth.

The world's largest source of nickel is at Sudbury, in Ontario, Canada. Nearly two billion years ago, an asteroid 7.5 miles (12 km) wide smashed into Earth's crust, traveling at 47 miles (75 km) a second. The area is still scarred by an oval crater 37 miles (60 km) across. Some of the nickel probably came from the asteroid itself as it vaporized (turned to gas) on impact. Most of the nickel probably flooded up from Earth's core in volcanic eruptions triggered by the asteroid's enormous impact.

DID YOU KNOW?

NICKEL IN SPACE

How did nickel end up in asteroids, meteorites, and the material that formed Earth? Scientists believe that it was formed in the cores of long-dead stars. Stars like the Sun shine by turning simple elements, such as hydrogen and helium, into heavier elements such as carbon and oxygen. Only the most massive stars—several times larger than the Sun—can make elements heavier than iron. These giant stars end their lives in massive explosions called supernovae. When a giant star becomes a supernova, it scatters its elements across space. The elements help to build the next generation of stars and planets.

Wherever nickel is found, it is stored away in mineral ores rather than pure metal nuggets. The most common ores are sulfides called pentlandite and pyrrhotite. Other nickel ores include niccolite, which contains poisonous arsenic, and laterites. Laterites are complex oxide compounds.

A piece of a meteorite from northern Australia which fell to Earth 4,700 years ago. Like most meteorites, this space rock was made up mainly of metals. About a tenth of this meteorite was pure nickel.

Mining and refining

ost nickel ores are either sulfides, such as pentlandite and pyrrhotite, or laterites, such as garnierite and limonite. The laterite ores are formed from the sulfide ones in a process called weathering. This involves water and carbon dioxide gas in the air changing the compound. Sulfide ores are found in volcanic rocks, and may lie close to the surface or be buried deep beneath it. Laterites are found mixed with other minerals. This mixture is found in rocks that are formed from layers of eroded sand and mud.

Mining methods

Different mining methods are used depending on the location of the nickel ore. For large amounts of sulfide buried deep below the ground, mining tunnels are dug and the seams of nickel-bearing rock are excavated. For ores closer to the surface, such as most laterites, it is easier to dig the rocks out from above, using heavy earthmoving machinery and explosives. This results in a huge hole called an open-pit mine. This hole can damage the environment unless it is carefully restored after the mining has ended.

As far as possible, rocks that do not contain nickel are separated from the ore at the mine site. Often, nickel deposits are found alongside other valuable metal ores, so these are sent for separate processing. The process of extracting the metal from the ore begins at a refinery.

Refining ores

The first stage of refining involves pulverizing the nickel-bearing rocks through a series of grinders and crushers, until it is reduced to grains less than 0.04

Trucks carry nickel ore out of a huge open-pit mine in South America.

inches (0.1 mm) across. Together, these fine particles have a very large surface area. This means that more of the nickel inside is exposed, and is more likely to undergo chemical reactions.

Sulfide ores are the simplest to process. The powdered ore is mixed with water, and air is bubbled through it. This causes the nickel sulfide particles to concentrate on the surface of the bubbles forming in the liquid. The particles rise to the top of the tank and form a frothy film that is then scraped off. By repeating the process many times, about 90 percent of the nickel sulfide can be extracted from the powder. The froth is then filtered and dried to create a powder of nickel sulfide.

To extract the pure nickel, the powder is smelted in a furnace. There the sulfides and the iron react with gases in the

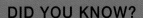

There are several stages to nickel purification. These tanks of water are used to separate nickel sulfide from impurities in powdered ore.

atmosphere and produce large amounts of heat. The result is a mixture of molten nickel that sinks to the bottom of the furnace, and slag (waste products) that floats to the top. The nickel is then removed and the process is repeated to extract as much nickel from the mix as possible. By the time the nickel has been refined to remove impurities, such as

DID YOU KNOW?

RECYCLING SCRAP

Because nickel is expensive to mine and process, it makes sense to recycle it. This is done generally by melting down objects containing nickel. The nickel is reused still mixed with other metals, rather than being purified again. Today, about one-third of the nickel used every year is recycled material. It could be more, but because nickel objects are resistant to corrosion they can be used for decades before they are ready for recycling.

Pure molten nickel is poured from a smelter at a refinery in South America. During smelting, impurities, such as sulfur, are burned away.

copper, the metal is 99.8 percent pure. This nickel may be purified still further by turning it into a carbonyl gas and burning the gas to release the nickel.

Oxide ores

For laterite ores, the process is very different, as the nickel is bound in much more complex compounds. For example, garnierite ore contains magnesium, silicon,

ATOMS AT WORK

Reduction of nickel sulfide

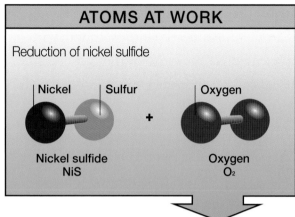

Nickel   Sulfur   +   Oxygen

Nickel sulfide
NiS

Oxygen
O_2

During the extraction process, nickel sulfide is converted to nickel by heating it in air.

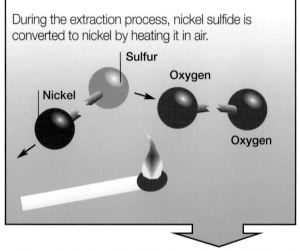

Sulfur

Oxygen

Nickel

Oxygen

Oxygen from the air reacts with the sulfur to form sulfur dioxide, leaving nickel behind.

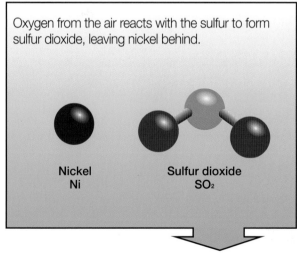

Nickel
Ni

Sulfur dioxide
SO_2

The reaction that takes place can be written like this:

$$NiS + O_2 \rightarrow Ni + SO_2$$

oxygen, and hydrogen, as well as nickel. The first stage in processing them is to dry out water in the crystals. Sulfur may be added to convert oxides into sulfides.

Another way to process these ores is called high-pressure acid leaching. A liquid made by mixing the powdered ore with water is heated to 536 °F (280 °C). It is

Nickel refineries, such as this one in South Africa, are generally close to the mine so the ore does not have to be transported far.

also kept at a high pressure to prevent the liquid from boiling. The mixture is then leached by pumping sulfuric acid through it. Nickel dissolves into the acid to form sulfides, which can then be extracted.

Some scientists are also experimenting with bacteria that feed on the impurities in laterites. In the future, microorganisms might be able to carry out at least the first stages of refining. The microorganisms could be used to process poisonous waste materials before disposal.

Nickel and its compounds

Nickel takes part in chemical reactions and forms compounds—larger molecules containing other elements. It does this to gain or lose electrons, making its shells as stable as possible. A stable atom is generally one with electron shells that are full or empty. Normally only the electrons in the outer shell are involved in reactions. In the transition metals, including nickel, the shell just inside the outermost one is also not completely full. Both shells, therefore, take part in reactions. This gives transition metals the ability to form very complex compounds.

Most of nickel's reactions involve losing two electrons from the outer shell. These electrons go to an atom that becomes more stable by gaining the electrons. Without the two negatively charged

These flasks hold a solution of complex ions that contain nickel. Each type of dissolved ion produces a different colored solution.

electrons, the nickel becomes an ion with a positive charge (Ni^{2+}). The atom that accepted the electrons forms a negative ion. The two ions are attracted to each other, forming an ionic bond.

When nickel in a compound has donated two electrons, it is said to have an oxidation state of +2. An example is nickel (II) sulfide. This is its most stable oxidation state, though nickel can form other states ranging from -1 to +4.

In normal conditions, nickel is unreactive. It is unaffected by most acids and also cannot be attacked by strong alkalis, such as sodium hydroxide. This makes nickel containers ideal for storing damaging and reactive materials.

Many pipes are coated with a thin layer of nickel. This prevents the pipe from corroding when reactive liquids and gases are pumped through them.

Complex ions

Because nickel and other transition metals have an incomplete inner shell as well, they can form a wider variety of compounds than most elements. Many of these are "complexes," in which the metal atom is surrounded by several identical groups of atoms, such as water (H_2O) or ammonia (NH_3). These surrounding groups, called ligands, are stable enough to exist on their own. However, they have pairs of electrons in their outer shells that are not otherwise being used in a bond.

ATOMS AT WORK

Nickel ions are dissolved in water.

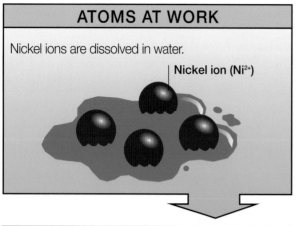

Nickel ion (Ni²⁺)

The electrons in the oxygen that make up the water molecules are attracted to the nickel ion.

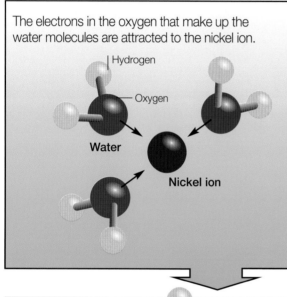

Hydrogen

Oxygen

Water

Nickel ion

The nickel ion and six water molecules form a complex ion called hexaquonickel (II).

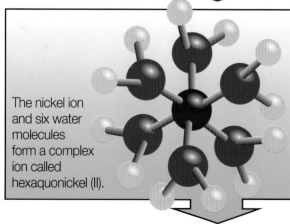

The reactions that take place can be written like this:

$$Ni^{2+} + 6H_2O \rightarrow Ni(H_2O)_6^{2+}$$

They can therefore donate both electrons to the nickel atom, forming another bond and stabilizing it.

Uses of pure nickel

Nickel's resistance to corrosion means it is often used to protect other metals. It is electroplated onto the surface of another metal to create a thin film. For example, it is used to line pipes that are going to be exposed to corrosive liquids.

Modern technology even allows plastics to be coated with a thin layer of metal that can then be electroplated with nickel. Nickel-coated plastic is used for chrome trims on cars, bathroom fittings, and electrical connectors. Nickel is also used in computer hard disks.

Nickel compounds at work

Before nickel was discovered, the people of northern Germany were already using nickel arsenide as a coloring for glass. Today, nickel oxides have similar uses in glassmaking and pottery glazing.

Nickel also has important uses in powering gadgets. For example, most small rechargeable batteries use nickel. These are called nickel-metal hydride batteries because they have a negative electrode made of nickel oxyhydroxide (NiOOH) and a positive one made of a metal hydride. They produce electricity by a chemical reaction that causes ions with

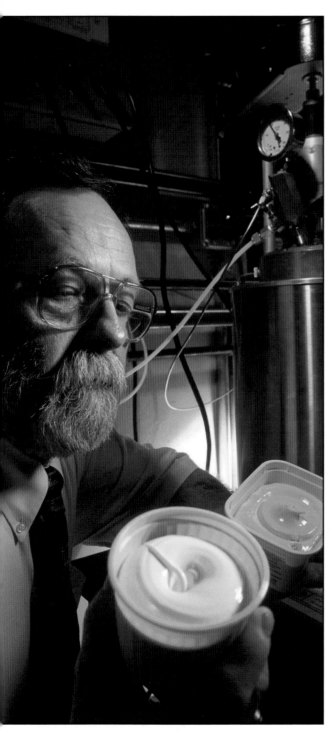

Nickel is used as a catalyst during the production of margarine. Liquid vegetable oil is turned into solid margarine by pumping hydrogen gas through it.

different charges to move between the electrons through a liquid. The liquid, or electrolyte, contains potassium hydroxide.

Nickel sulfate is an important mordant. Mordants are chemicals that make a color from another chemical stick to cloth in a dyeing process. In the future, nickel may become very important because of its ability to collect large amounts of hydrogen gas, forming nickel hydride. Nickel and other metal hydrides could be the key to a new generation of pollution-free, hydrogen-powered fuel cells. Hydrides can store more hydrogen atoms than even liquid hydrogen can, and they are easier to handle. Engineers are looking for ways to release the hydrogen from the hydrides efficiently.

Nickel in steel

The main use for nickel is in making steel. Steel is a strong metal that has a huge range of uses in modern technology and industry. Steel is a metal mixture, or alloy, in which hot liquid iron is mixed with one or more other elements. When the steel is allowed to cool and set, the atoms form a crystalline network or lattice. Having even small amounts of other atoms mixed in with the iron can give steel dramatically different properties, such as making it resistant to rust, or giving it added strength.

Steel containing nickel is resistant to corrosion and is more ductile. It was first used in armor plate, invented by British engineer James Riley in 1889. Riley found that iron plating could be made stronger

Stainless steel is a shiny alloy that does not rust. It is used in cutlery and other cooking equipment. Nickel is an essential ingredient of stainless steel. Stainless steel is mainly iron, but it also contains carbon and chromium.

DID YOU KNOW?

HOW STEEL IS MADE

The basic principles of large-scale steel manufacture have not changed since they were discovered by English industrialist Henry Bessemer (1813–1898) in the 1850s. Ingots of impure iron are melted in a furnace with limestone chunks. Oxygen is blown through the molten mixture. Impurities in the iron react with the oxygen and are blown out of the furnace. Carefully controlled amounts of the other elements required in the steel are added to the molten mixture. The molten steel is then allowed to flow into ingots, which can be melted again and passed through heavy rollers to make sheets of steel.

and firmer by adding chromium and nickel. The resulting alloy was very strong and resistant to heat. Used to make armor for tanks and battleships, this invention paved the way for the mechanized warfare of the twentieth century.

The most common use for nickel today is in stainless steel, a shiny type of steel that is resistant to attack by corrosive

A modern battle tank is armored with thick plates of steel. The steel contains a high proportion of nickel, which makes it very strong.

chemicals. Most stainless steels are around 18 percent chromium and 8 percent nickel, often with the addition of a little molybdenum or other elements. The chromium forms a thin layer of corrosion-resistant chromium oxide as it cools after the manufacturing process. This oxide layer protects the alloy from the outside world. Even when the metal is scratched, the oxide layer "heals" itself. The nickel helps to stabilize the outer layer and also makes the steel easier to work than a chromium-iron blend alone.

Other steels containing nickel are used for structures that will be pulled on regularly. A ductile material is better than one that will remain completely rigid and break suddenly. Nickel steels are used in everything from bridge construction to bicycle chains.

Nickel is also frequently used in modern steels designed to operate at very low temperatures. It is ideal for storing liquefied gases such as hydrogen, helium, and nitrogen. Another nickel steel, called maraging steel, contains nickel, cobalt, titanium, and molybdenum. It is twice as hard as stainless steel or titanium and is used in rocket fuel tanks and golf clubs.

HISTORY OF STAINLESS STEEL

The first stainless steels were made in the English city of Sheffield around 1912 by Harry Brearley, head of the Brown Firth steel laboratories. He discovered the steels by accident, while investigating the properties of various mixes of iron and chromium. However, the alloy he created contained no nickel. It had a high melting point and was remarkably hard and resistant to corrosion. The following year, chemists at the German firm Krupps had the idea of adding nickel to create a softer alloy that could be made into objects more easily.

Steel containing nickel is used to make the tough clubs used to hit golf balls.

Other nickel alloys

Apart from its use in steel, nickel is a part of many other important alloys that have a wide variety of uses. It is most often combined with chromium to make temperature-resistant alloys, or with copper to make corrosion-resistant ones.

Heat and stress

Chromium-nickel alloys remain strong at incredibly high temperatures and have a huge range of uses. Spark plugs in internal-combustion engines and heating elements in electric fires and stoves are a few examples of how these alloys are used.

Nickel alloys are used in jet engines. The fan blades inside the jet are subjected to extreme heat and enormous stresses as they spin. If one were to break, the result would be disastrous. Turbine blades were once made of steel, but would weaken at high temperatures. Since nickel has a very high melting point, an alloy made with 75 percent of the metal actually gets stronger as temperatures increase. Modern nickel turbines can operate at much higher speeds and temperatures.

Chemical attacks

Copper-nickel alloys are not as strong as chromium-nickel ones but can resist a wider range of chemical attacks. This

A turbofan jet engine is fitted to the wing of a passenger jet. The curved blades of the fan and other moving parts of the engine contain nickel.

makes them ideal for use in marine engineering. One useful alloy is called monel metal. It is a mix of 67 percent nickel, 30 percent copper, and small amounts of other elements. The resulting shiny, resistant metal is used for ships' propellers and other fittings that will be exposed to salty seawater. Related alloys are used for covering underwater cables and in desalination plants where seawater is turned into fresh water.

Alloying nickel with around 36 percent iron produces invar, which has a unique property that gives it a huge range of uses. Most metals expand a lot as they heat up, and shrink when they cool. This can cause problems in precisely engineered devices.

The huge monal-metal propeller of the icebreaker S. S. Manhattan is swung into position.

Invar has the lowest rate of expansion across a huge range of temperatures, from –148 °F to 392 °F (–100 °C to 200 °C).

This makes it ideal for making television components, for example. Invar is also used in water heaters, kettles, and central-heating controls, where it forms one half of the bimetallic strip thermostat. These work by having a strip of invar attached to another metal strip that expands more rapidly with rising temperature. As the two metals heat up, one strip expands more than the other. The whole unit, therefore, begins to bend (see diagram on the right). Inside thermostats the moving strip acts as a switch to turn heaters and refrigerators on or off.

Magnetism

Nickel's magnetic properties make it a useful material for magnets. When alloyed with aluminum and cobalt it forms alnico, a highly magnetic material. Unlike other magnets, alnico magnets stay magnetic even at very high temperatures. Alnico is used for scientific instruments and meters, communications equipment, generators, and inside gas turbines.

Mu metal is another magnetic alloy of nickel, and has very special properties. Its mix of 77 percent nickel, 15 percent iron, plus copper and molybdenum, gives it a very low magnetic permeability. This means mu metal acts as a barrier to magnetic fields. The ability to isolate an area from artificial or natural magnetism can be very useful in laboratories.

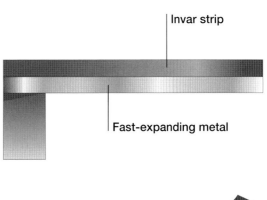

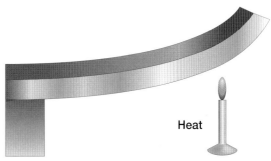

Invar alloy, which contains nickel, is used in bimetallic strips. When the strip heats up, the invar strip expands more slowly than the other one. The other strip becomes longer than the invar one, and the two strips begin to bend upwards. If the device was cooled, the strips would bend the other way.

DID YOU KNOW?

SMART MATERIALS
Probably the most amazing nickel alloys are the ones that form when nickel is mixed with tungsten. Together, the atoms of the two metals form a "shape memory" alloy. They form a certain shape at a particular temperature. The metal atoms "remember" that shape and return to it when they are returned to that temperature, even if they have changed shape while being cooled or heated.

Nickel coins

Most of us will come into daily contact with nickel in the form of coins. The U.S. five-cent piece is even nicknamed the "nickel." However, the United States was not the first country to use nickel in its currency. Nickel was used in coin alloys by several ancient cultures. The first modern nickel coins were produced in Switzerland in 1850.

Inexpensive metal

In most cultures, coins started out as tokens made from precious metals, such as gold or silver. The value of each coin was related to the weight of metal it contained. As precious metals became more valuable, the coins had to get smaller to make them useful for inexpensive purchases. Eventually, someone had the idea of making coins that had no real value, but simply represented an amount of money. The first of these coins were made from copper, but they bent and corroded easily. Once it was discovered, the alloy of zinc, copper, and nickel, known as nickel-silver, proved to be better coin material. It did not corrode or bend very easily, and it could be mixed with other metals to produce gold-, silver-, and bronze-colored coins.

A U.S. five-cent piece, or nickel. The coin is a mixture of copper and nickel metal. Nickels were first minted in 1866. Early versions showed a bison and Native American. The design on the left was used from 1938 until 2004, when the latest designs were introduced.

Nickel and the body

The human body contains about 10 milligrams of nickel. The element is found in many foods. Walnuts are one of the richest sources of nickel. The kidneys control the amount of nickel in the body, but scientists do not know exactly why.

Nickel is used in digestive enzymes, chemicals that help break down food, used by several animals. A shortage of nickel slows the development of many other animals. In humans, it could be involved in digesting sugar, and might trigger the production of breast milk. It is also present in ribonucleic acid (RNA), a chemical that helps to build the proteins that make up our cells and bodies.

DID YOU KNOW?

NICKEL ALLERGIES

Many people have an allergy to nickel called "nickel itch." They break out in a rash and can even have more serious reactions. The allergy develops when someone becomes "sensitized" by having regular contact with nickel objects. This was more common in the past, when inexpensive jewelry was nickel plated. Chemicals in sweat from the body reacts with nickel to produce salts that irritate the skin. Recently, it was discovered that many of the Euro coins used as the new European currency contained too much nickel. But few people have had skin problems after handling the coins.

The rash on this girl's neck is caused by the nickel in a necklace she was wearing. The rash is treated with creams and drugs called corticosteroids.

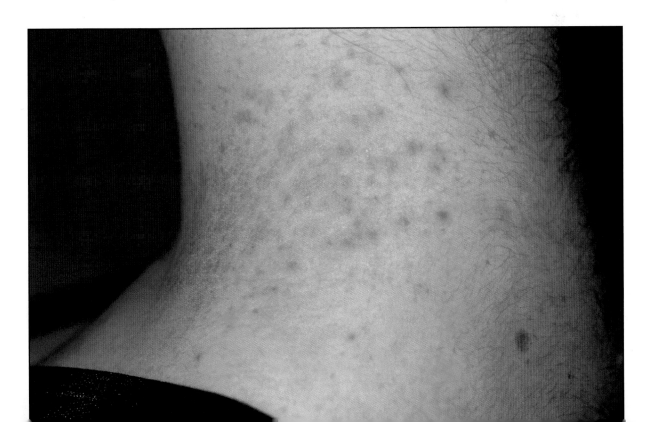

Periodic table

Everything in the universe is made from combinations of substances called elements. Elements are the building blocks of matter. They are made of tiny atoms, which are too small to see.

The character of an atom depends on how many even tinier particles called protons there are in its center, or nucleus. An element's atomic number is the same as the number of protons.

Scientists have found around 110 different elements. About 90 elements occur naturally on Earth. The rest have been made in experiments.

All these elements are set out on a chart called the periodic table. This lists all the elements in order according to their atomic number.

The elements at the left of the table are metals. Those at the right are nonmetals. Between the metals and the nonmetals are the metalloids, which sometimes act like metals and sometimes like nonmetals.

● On the left of the table are the alkali metals. These elements have just one electron in their outer shells.

● On the right of the periodic table are the noble gases. These elements have full outer shells.

● Elements in the same group have the same number of electrons in their outer shells.

● Elements get more reactive as you go down a group.

● The number of electrons orbiting the nucleus increases down each group.

● The transition metals are in the middle of the table, between Groups II and III.

Group I

Group II

Transition metals

Group I	Group II							
1 **H** Hydrogen 1								
3 **Li** Lithium 7	4 **Be** Beryllium 9							
11 **Na** Sodium 23	12 **Mg** Magnesium 24							
19 **K** Potassium 39	20 **Ca** Calcium 40	21 **Sc** Scandium 45	22 **Ti** Titanium 48	23 **V** Vanadium 51	24 **Cr** Chromium 52	25 **Mn** Manganese 55	26 **Fe** Iron 56	27 **Co** Cobalt 59
37 **Rb** Rubidium 85	38 **Sr** Strontium 88	39 **Y** Yttrium 89	40 **Zr** Zirconium 91	41 **Nb** Niobium 93	42 **Mo** Molybdenum 96	43 **Tc** Technetium (98)	44 **Ru** Ruthenium 101	45 **Rh** Rhodium 103
55 **Cs** Cesium 133	56 **Ba** Barium 137	71 **Lu** Lutetium 175	72 **Hf** Hafnium 179	73 **Ta** Tantalum 181	74 **W** Tungsten 184	75 **Re** Rhenium 186	76 **Os** Osmium 190	77 **Ir** Iridium 192
87 **Fr** Francium 223	88 **Ra** Radium 226	103 **Lr** Lawrencium (260)	104 **Unq** Unniiquadium (261)	105 **Unp** Unnilpentium (262)	106 **Unh** Unnilhexium (263)	107 **Uns** Unnilseptium (?)	108 **Uno** Unniloctium (?)	109 **Une** Unilenium (?)

Lanthanide elements

Actinide elements

57 **La** Lanthanum 39	58 **Ce** Cerium 140	59 **Pr** Praseodymium 141	60 **Nd** Neodymium 144	61 **Pm** Promethium (145)
89 **Ac** Actinium 227	90 **Th** Thorium 232	91 **Pa** Protactinium 231	92 **U** Uranium 238	93 **Np** Neptunium (237)

The horizontal rows are called periods. As you go across a period, the atomic number increases by one from each element to the next. The vertical columns are called groups. Elements get heavier as you go down a group. All the elements in a group have the same number of electrons in their outer shells. This means they react in similar ways.

The transition metals fall between Groups II and III. Their electron shells fill up in an unusual way. The lanthanide elements and the actinide elements are set apart from the main table to make it easier to read. All the lanthanide elements and the actinide elements are quite rare.

Nickel in the table

Nickel is in the first period of the transition metals. Like other transition metals, nickel atoms have empty spaces in both their two outermost electron shells. This allows them to form a range of complex ions, which can have a variety of charges. Nickel compounds come in several vibrant colors, especially blue and green.

Metals

Metalloids (semimetals)

Nonmetals

								Group VIII
								2 He Helium 4
28 Ni Nickel 59 — Atomic (proton) number, Symbol, Name, Atomic mass			Group III	Group IV	Group V	Group VI	Group VII	
			5 B Boron 11	6 C Carbon 12	7 N Nitrogen 14	8 O Oxygen 16	9 F Fluorine 19	10 Ne Neon 20
			13 Al Aluminum 27	14 Si Silicon 28	15 P Phosphorus 31	16 S Sulfur 32	17 Cl Chlorine 35	18 Ar Argon 40
28 Ni Nickel 59	29 Cu Copper 64	30 Zn Zinc 65	31 Ga Gallium 70	32 Ge Germanium 73	33 As Arsenic 75	34 Se Selenium 79	35 Br Bromine 80	36 Kr Krypton 84
46 Pd Palladium 106	47 Ag Silver 108	48 Cd Cadmium 112	49 In Indium 115	50 Sn Tin 119	51 Sb Antimony 122	52 Te Tellurium 128	53 I Iodine 127	54 Xe Xenon 131
78 Pt Platinum 195	79 Au Gold 197	80 Hg Mercury 201	81 Tl Thallium 204	82 Pb Lead 207	83 Bi Bismuth 209	84 Po Polonium (209)	85 At Astatine (210)	86 Rn Radon (222)

62 Sm Samarium 150	63 Eu Europium 152	64 Gd Gadolinium 157	65 Tb Terbium 159	66 Dy Dysprosium 163	67 Ho Holmium 165	68 Er Erbium 167	69 Tm Thulium 169	70 Yb Ytterbium 173
94 Pu Plutonium (244)	95 Am Americium (243)	96 Cm Curium (247)	97 Bk Berkelium (247)	98 Cf Californium (251)	99 Es Einsteinium (252)	100 Fm Fermium (257)	101 Md Mendelevium (258)	102 No Nobelium (259)

Chemical reactions

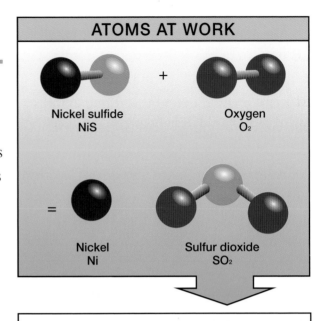

Chemical reactions are going on around us all the time. Some reactions involve just two substances; others many more. But whenever a reaction takes place, at least one substance is changed.

In a chemical reaction, the atoms stay the same. But they join up in different combinations to form new molecules.

Writing an equation

Chemical reactions can be described by writing down the atoms and molecules before and after the reactions.

The reaction that takes place when nickel sulfide reacts with oxygen is written like this:

$$NiS + O_2 \rightarrow Ni + SO_2$$

This tells us that one molecule of nickel sulfide reacts with one molecule of oxygen to make one atom of nickel and one molecule of sulfur dioxide.

Chunks of purified nickel are produced at a refinery in Australia. Nickel is mixed with other metals to make heat- and rust-resistant objects.

Since the atoms always stay the same, the number of atoms before the reaction will be the same as the number of atoms after it. Chemists write the reaction as an equation. This shows what happens in the chemical reaction.

Making it balance

When the numbers of each atom on both sides of the equation are equal, the equation is balanced. If the numbers are not equal, something is wrong. The chemist adjusts the number of atoms involved until the equation balances.

Glossary

atom: The smallest part of an element having all the properties of that element. Each atom is less than a millionth of an inch in diameter.

atomic mass: The mass of the protons, neutrons, and electrons in an atom.

atomic number: The number of protons in an atom.

bond: The attraction between two atoms or ions that holds them together.

compound: A substance made of atoms of two or more elements. The atoms are held together by chemical bonds.

corrosion: The eating away of a material by reaction with other chemicals, often oxygen and moisture in the air.

crystal: A solid consisting of a repeating pattern of atoms, ions, or molecules.

electrode: A material through which an electrical current flows into, or out of, a liquid electrolyte.

electron: A tiny particle with a negative charge. Electrons are found inside atoms, where they move around the nucleus in layers called electron shells.

electrolyte: A liquid that electricity can flow through.

element: A substance that is made from only one type of atom. Nickel belongs to a large series of elements known as the transition metals.

ion: A particle of an element similar to an atom but carrying an additional negative or positive electrical charge.

laterite: An ore containing nickel oxide.

ligand: An ion or molecule that joins to a transition metal to form a complex ion.

magnetism: A property of nickel, iron, and cobalt that produces forces which pull the metals together or push them apart.

metal: An element on the left-hand side of the periodic table.

mineral: A compound or element as it is found in its natural form in Earth.

molecule: A unit that contains atoms held together by chemical bonds.

neutron: A tiny particle with no electrical charge found in the nucleus of an atom.

niccolite: A mineral containing nickel and arsenic, also called kupfernickel.

nucleus: The center of an atom. It contains protons and neutrons

ore: A rock that contains a mineral mixed up with other substances.

periodic table: A chart of all the chemical elements laid out in order of their atomic number.

proton: A tiny particle with a positive charge. Protons are found inside the nucleus of an atom.

transition metal: An element positioned in the middle of the periodic table. As well as having spaces in their outer electron shell, transition metals also have spaces in the next shell in.

Index